AND GAMES

How to play more than 70 of the world's greatest games for two or more players

JOE GANNON

Mud Puddle Books
NEW YORK

Fun & Games:
How to play more than 70 of the world's greatest games
for two or more players
by Joe Gannon

© 2006 by Mud Puddle Books, Inc.

Mud Puddle Books, Inc.
54 W. 21st Street
Suite 601
New York, NY 10010
info@mudpuddlebooks.com

ISBN: 1-59412-154-0

All rights reserved. No part of this book may be reproduced or transmitted in any form or by any means, electronic or mechanical, including photocopying, recording, or by any information storage and retrieval system, without permission in writing from the publisher.

Book design by Mulberry Tree Press, Inc.

Printed and bound in China

Contents

Introduction • 4
Sidewalk Chalk • 5
  Basic Hopscotch • 6
  Classic Hopscotch • 9
  English Hopscotch • 10
  Tic-Tac-Hopscotch • 11
  Swamp Hopscotch • 12
  Eleven-Points • 13
  Snail • 14
  Ladder • 15
  Tic-Tac-Toss • 16
  Chalk Toss • 17
  Tic-Tac-Toe • 18
  Hangman • 19
  Dots • 20
Footbag • 21
  Basic Kicks • 22
  Competitive Footbag Games • 23
    Footbag Consecutive Games • 23
      Singles • 23
      Doubles • 23
      Doubles One-Pass • 24
      Speed Consecutive Doubles • 24
      Speed Consecutive
        Doubles One-Pass • 24
    Distance One-Pass • 25
    One-Up Five-Down • 25
    Team • 25
  Other Footbag Games • 26
    Hackball • 26
    Copycat • 26
    Round Robin • 27
    Elimination • 27
Marbles • 28
  Lagging • 28
  Shooters and Mibs • 29
  Funsies and Keepsies • 29
  Ringer • 30
  Ring Taw • 31
  Boss Out • 32
  Dropsies • 33
  Potsies • 34
  Tic-Tac-Toe • 35

Jacks • 36
  Flipping • 36
  Basic Jacks: Plainsies • 37
  Options to Make the Game Easier • 38
  Fancies • 39
    Eggs in the Basket • 39
    Pigs in the Pen • 39
    Scrubs • 40
    Sheep over the Fence • 40
    Goats on the Mountain • 40
    Speed Jacks • 41
    Marble Jacks • 41
Chinese Jump Rope • 42
  Americans • 43
  Skinny Americans • 46
  Diamonds • 50
  Sailboats • 53
  Chinese • 57
  Snap Back • 60
Tag & Other Fun Games • 62
  Picking Who Is "It" • 63
  Tag • 64
  Grab Tag • 65
  Freeze Tag • 66
  Pie Tag • 67
  Rabbit • 68
  Octopus • 69
  Hide and Seek • 70
  Arm Wrestling • 71
  Hand Wrestling • 72
  Marco Polo • 73
  Duck Duck Goose • 74
  Mother May I • 75
  Red Light – Green Light • 76
  Blind Man's Bluff • 77
  Red Rover • 78
  Simon Says • 79
  Rock – Paper – Scissors • 80

Introduction

These days, with game systems and computerized video games all around us, it's easy to forget that kids have been playing games since the dawn of civilization. Often using little more than their imagination they've always found ways to have fun. Try a few of the games in this volume and I think you'll see that the simplest of pleasures are often the finest, and you don't have to haul a pile of equipment along with you to have a great time with your friends.

Sidewalk Chalk

Let the pavement be your game board. Hopscotch has been around since the Romans ruled Britain. There, it was practiced on huge courts as an exercise for training the footwork of the Roman Legions. Children imitated the soldiers and drew their own smaller courts to play on. From Britain it spread across Europe and around the world, developing countless variations, and continues its popularity through today. Pen and paper games can also be amusing when scaled up to supersized asphalt versions.

Basic Hopscotch

❶ Draw a Basic Hopscotch board in chalk on the pavement following the diagram here.

❷ During the game, players may not land on a line or outside of the box they intend to land in. When hopping, they must remain on the same foot and the other foot may not touch the ground, except where it is specified that they should land on both feet.

❸ A player may not land in a square that contains any player's marker, including his own. He must jump over it. On his return trip down the board he must stop and pick up his marker, which then allows him to land in the square that it had occupied.

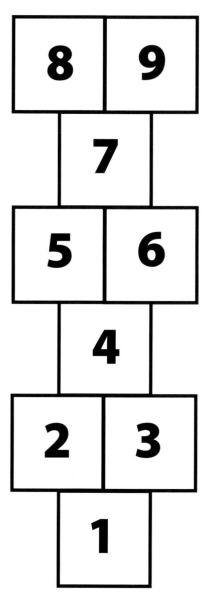

❹ The first player drops his marker (also called a "potsie") on the *one* square. A footbag makes a distinctive hopscotch marker. The marker must land completely within the lines that define the square and not touching any of them. If it does not, the player's turn is over.

❺ He then hops over the *one* square and lands on two feet, with his left foot in the *two* square and his right in the *three* square; then hops on one foot into the *four* square; then again hops landing on two feet, with his left foot in the *five* square and his right in the *six* square: then hops on one foot into the *seven* square; and again hops landing on two feet, with his left in the *eight* square and his right in the *nine* square.

❻ He then jumps up and turns in the air landing on two feet again, but this time with his right foot in the *eight* square and his left in the *nine* square.

❼ He proceeds back down the board, hopping on one foot in the *seven* square; landing on two feet, with his right in the *five* square and his *left* in the six square; then hopping on one foot in the *four* square; two feet in the *two* and *three* squares, and finally on one foot in the *one* square before hopping off the board.

❽ On the return trip down the board, the player stops to pick up his marker before jumping into the *one* square that contained it. After hopping off the board he tosses his marker into the next square, the *two* square, where it will remain until his next turn.

❾ Player two throws her marker into the *one* square. She must then hop landing on one foot in the *three* square, skipping both the one and two squares, because they contain markers.

❿ She then proceeds up and then back down the board in the same manner described above.

⓫ The players take turns hopping up and down the board. In any turn that he makes a mistake—missing the correct square when throwing his marker, landing on a line, touching down with the wrong foot, or jumping in a square that contains a marker—his turn is over and he does not advance.

⓬ If a marker occupies one square in a pair of squares that would normally be landed in with both feet, the player hops on the appropriate single foot in the one square which is still available. If both are occupied the player hops over them to the next square in the sequence.

⓭ The first player to advance his or her marker to the eight square is the winner.

Option: The board may have a "home" square at the top of the board, after squares eight and nine, where players may rest before they hop back down the board.

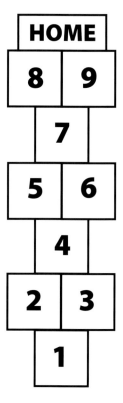

Classic Hopscotch

Classic Hopscotch follows the same rules as Basic Hopscotch but uses a slightly different board as shown here, and therefore, it also has a somewhat different hopping sequence:

❶ Hop on two feet in squares one and two.

❷ Hop on one foot in square three.

❸ Hop on two feet in squares four and five.

❹ Hop on one foot in squares six and seven.

❺ Hop on two feet in squares eight and nine.

❻ Hop on one foot in square ten.

❼ Land on two feet in eleven.

❽ Turn and land on two feet again in eleven.

❾ Come back down the board, reversing the pattern.

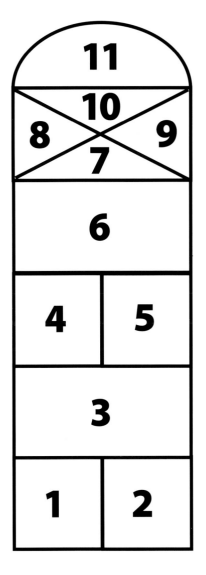

The game is won by advancing your marker to segment eleven.

English Hopscotch

❶ English Hopscotch uses a distinctly different board shown here. Draw the board in chalk on the pavement.

❷ A large marker is required since the player must hop with both legs, and hold the marker between his legs while hopping without dropping it.

❸ Squares are hopped from one to six sequentially, and both feet must land entirely within the next square. If he lands fully within a square, he can attempt to hop to the next square, but must do so from precisely where he landed.

❹ If a player fails to hop cleanly onto the next square his turn is over, but on his subsequent turn he may begin from anywhere within the highest square that he reached cleanly on his last turn.

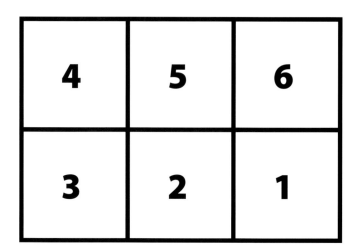

Tic-Tac-Hopscotch

❶ Use the Classic Hopscotch board drawn in chalk on the pavement.

❷ The player hops through all of the segments on one foot in sequence. There are no two foot landings in this game.

❸ When she has successfully hopped up and back down the board, the first player may mark her initials in any segment she chooses. The other players may no longer land on that segment.

❹ The next player proceeds up and down the board, avoiding the segment that has been initialed by his opponent. If he is successful in completing the board he may mark a segment with his initials.

❺ During play, no player may land on a segment marked with an opponent's initials, but on subsequent trips up and down the board players are allowed to stop on their own segments landing there on two feet to rest.

❻ As the board fills up with initials it will eventually become impassable. At that point the player with the most initials on the board is the winner.

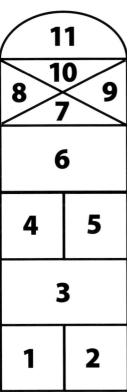

Swamp Hopscotch

❶ Swamp is played on the board shown in the diagram here.

❷ The player must first hop through squares 1 to 14 on one foot without landing on a line or in the swamp (the middle).

❸ Then the player must hop backwards one foot back to one.

❹ The player must then hop on two feet from square 1 to 14.

❺ And then the player must hop backwards on two feet back to square one.

❻ Any time a player lands on a line or in the swamp her turn is over.

❼ On her next turn she may pick up from the square where she last made an error.

❽ The first player to cleanly complete both passes through the boxes is the winner. You will find that jumping backwards without landing on a line is harder than you might think.

12	13	14	1
11	The		2
10	Swamp		3
9			4
8	7	6	5

Eleven-Points

1 In chalk on the pavement, draw the board shown in the diagram here. The horizontal lines in the diagrams are like the rungs of a ladder. You gain one point for each "rung" of the ladder that you cross during the game.

2 Each player jumps as far as possible from the start line and puts down a marker where she lands.

3 On the next turn each player jumps as far as she can from where her marker is.

4 When the player gets to the goal she gets 11 points and starts over at the beginning.

5 The first player to reach 100 points is the winner.

Snail

❶ Draw the Snail board as shown in the diagram here.

❷ On the first pass through the player hops in every segment from 1 to home and back.

❸ On the second pass through the board the player hops in every other segment: 1, 3, 5, 7, 9, home, and back again, still landing in every other segment.

❹ On the third pass he hops in every third segment, and so on.

❺ The player who can stay in the game the longest without an error is the winner.

Ladder

❶ Draw the Ladder board in chalk on the pavement as shown in the diagram here.

❷ Ladder is played in the same way as Snail: first jump up and back through the squares using every box.

❸ On the second round use every other box; on the third round, every third box; and so on.

❹ Again, the player who survives the longest is the winner.

Tic-Tac-Toss

❶ Draw a large tic-tac-toe grid in chalk on the pavement, two foot (61 cm) squares make a nice grid. The larger the grid, the easier the game will be.

❷ Draw a shooting line on the pavement several feet away from the grid, about six feet (2 m) is a good distance. The farther away the shooting line is, the harder the game becomes.

❸ Players take turns tossing a marker and trying to land it in an available square on the grid. A footbag makes a great marker for tossing.

❹ If the marker stops completely within an available square of the grid, the thrower marks her initials in the square in chalk and she "owns" that square making it unavailable to the other players.

❺ The winner is the first player to own three squares in a line: horizontal, vertical, or diagonal.

❻ For a more challenging variation you can add squares to the grid, making it 4 x 4, or 5 x 5.

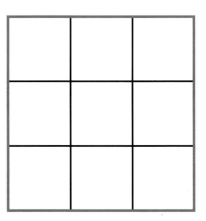

SHOOTING LINE

Chalk Toss

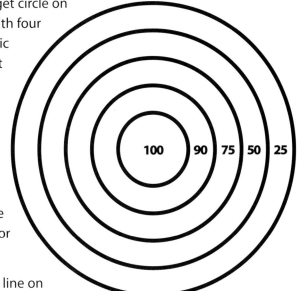

❶ Draw a large target circle on the pavement with four smaller concentric circles inside of it as shown in the diagram.

❷ Mark the point values in each of the bands of the target with the highest value being awarded for a bull's-eye.

❸ Draw a shooting line on the pavement several feet away from the target, about six feet (2 m) is a good distance. The farther away the shooting line is, the harder the game becomes.

❹ Players take turns tossing a marker onto the target. A footbag makes a great marker for tossing.

❺ The goal is to land the marker as near to the bull's-eye as possible. Players are awarded the number of points marked on the section within which the marker lands.

❻ The first player to score a total of 200 points wins.

❼ For an alternative you can try drawing the target differently. Use the one shown here or make up your own.

Tic-Tac-Toe

❶ Draw the tic-tac-toe grid in chalk on the pavement as shown in the diagram.

❷ The first player draws an O in any square of the grid.

❸ The second player draws an X in any of the open squares.

❹ Play continues with the players alternately adding Os and Xs to the open squares of the grid.

❺ The goal is to get three in a row (up, down, or diagonally) while blocking your opponent from getting three in a row.

❻ If all the squares are filled and neither player has three in a row the game is a tie.

❼ For a more challenging variation you can add squares to the grid, making it 4 x 4, or 5 x 5.

Hangman

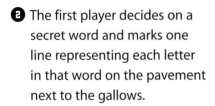

① Draw a gallows in chalk on the pavement like the one in the diagram here.

② The first player decides on a secret word and marks one line representing each letter in that word on the pavement next to the gallows.

③ The second player tries to guess the letters in the word.

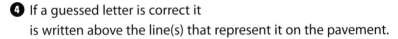

④ If a guessed letter is correct it is written above the line(s) that represent it on the pavement.

⑤ If a guessed letter is incorrect a piece is added to the stick figure on the gallows. First a head is drawn. With each incorrect guess another piece is added: next is the body, then an arm, the other arm, a leg, the other leg, a foot, and lastly the other foot— always in that order.

⑥ Keep track of the incorrect guesses by writing them down on any open stretch of pavement.

⑦ The object is to guess the word before the stick figure is complete.

⑧ If the guesser figures out the word before the stick figure is complete they get to select the next word and the players' roles are reversed. If not, the first player selects a new secret word and the guesser gets to try again.

Dots

❶ Make a square grid of dots on the pavement using the chalk. It may be as large or small as you'd like—larger grids are more challenging.

❷ Players take turns adding lines to the grid connecting pairs of dots. Lines may be horizontal or vertical but they can NOT be diagonal.

❸ If the line that a player adds completes a square using lines that are already drawn, that player puts his initial in the square and then gets to add another line. His turn continues as long as each line he adds completes a square. After the final square he completes, he MUST add another line.

❹ When all of the squares are completed the game is over, and the player with his initial in the highest number of squares is the winner.

❺ For an interesting challenge, try making the grid in some shape other than a square.

Footbag

Footbag is played with a round object about two inches (5 cm) in diameter, usually crocheted or made of hand sewn leather and filled with plastic beads. The basic object of the game is to keep the footbag off of the ground using only the feet and legs. Although the roots of footbag can be traced back over four thousand years to ancient China, modern American footbag was developed in Oregon in 1972 by John Stalberger and Mike Marshal who were trying to come up with an activity that would strengthen John's injured knee. A patent was granted to John in 1979 and in 1983 Wham-O bought the rights to manufacture and distribute the footbag in North America under the now well-known name of Hacky Sack.® In 1983 the World Footbag Association was formed to promote the sport, encourage development, and standardize the rules. Its popularity continues to grow with each passing year.

Basic Kicks

There are three main kicks used in footbag:

Inside kick: Swing the leg to the inside, toward the opposite leg. Strike the footbag with the inside of the foot. The foot should come to knee high or higher before the strike. The strike should be made with the side of the arch below the ankle. Turn your ankle in and curl the foot and toes to present a flatter striking surface.

Outside kick: Swing the leg to the outside, away from opposite leg. Strike with the outside of the foot at knee level or above. The strike should be made with the middle of the outside of the foot below the ankle. Point the toes to present a flatter striking surface.

Back kick: Swing the leg back striking the footbag at or above knee level. Rotate the toes outward and point them to present a flatter striking surface on the outside of the foot, similar to the outside kick. Rotate the upper body toward the striking leg so that you can see the footbag when you strike it.

There are also two minor kicks, used only when absolutely necessary :

Toe kick: Flip the footbag up with the top of the toes. It should only be used to set up one of the main kicks, or to save a footbag that has fallen too low to execute one of the main kicks.

Knee kick: Bump the footbag up using the top surface of the knee or lower thigh. It is generally used as a block to keep the footbag from hitting the body.

Competitive Footbag Games
sanctioned by the IFPA (International Footbag Players' Association)

Footbag Consecutive Games

Footbag consecutive games can be played with one or more players who's object is to keep the footbag in the air using only the feet and knees. Score is kept by keeping track of how many times the footbag is struck before a drop or a foul occurs, or within an allotted time period, depending on the type of game being played.

The player must kick the footbag—catching the footbag on the foot or leg is not allowed. A kick must be comprised of a continuous striking motion. The kicker cannot support himself by contact with any structure or object when kicking. It is a foul if the footbag contacts any surface other than the player or if the footbag makes any contact with the upper body (above the waist), including contact with clothing or other equipment. The player must begin each rally with a hand serve.

Singles

An individual player tries to keep the footbag in the air as long as he can. A point is awarded for each kick of the footbag. The rally is over when the footbag touches the ground or a foul occurs.

Doubles

Two players try to keep the footbag in the air as long they can. Each player is allowed up to 25 consecutive kicks before passing the footbag. A point is awarded for each kick of the footbag. The rally is over when the footbag touches the ground or a foul occurs, or when one of the players makes more than 25 consecutive strikes of the footbag.

Doubles One-Pass

Two players try to keep the footbag in the air as long they can. Each is allowed only one kick of the footbag on his turn. The footbag passes back and forth between the players with each kick. A point is awarded for each kick of the footbag. The rally is over when the footbag touches the ground or a foul occurs, or when one of the players makes more than one consecutive strike of the footbag.

Speed Consecutive Singles

An individual player tries to kick the footbag as many times as he can within an allotted period of time, usually five minutes. Players must alternate legs with each kick. A point is awarded for each kick of the footbag. If the footbag leaves the player's hand before the time is started a deduction of 10 points is made. The rally continues if the footbag touches the ground or a foul occurs, but the following deductions are made: 3 points for a non-alternating-foot foul, and 10 points for a drop or upper-body foul. The rally is over when the allotted time is up.

Speed Consecutive Doubles One-Pass

Two players try to kick the footbag as many times as they can within an allotted period of time, usually five minutes. Each is allowed only one kick of the footbag on his turn. The footbag passes back and forth between the players with each kick. A point is awarded for each kick of the footbag. The rally is over if any of the following occurs: the footbag leaves the starting player's hand before the time is started, the footbag touches the ground, an upper-body foul occurs, or one of the players makes more than one consecutive strike of the footbag.

Distance One Pass

Two players try to pass the footbag across a 10 foot (3 m) distance as many times as they can. Each is allowed only one kick of the footbag on his turn. The footbag passes back and forth between the players with each kick. Lines (at least two inches [5 cm] wide) are drawn on the ground 10 feet (3 m) apart and if a player touches the ground beyond the line it is a foul, ending the rally. A point is awarded for each kick of the footbag. The rally is over when the footbag touches the ground or a foul occurs, or when one of the players makes more than one consecutive strike of the footbag. Each pair is allowed three rallies and is awarded the best score of the three attempts.

One-up Five-down

Two players try to keep the footbag in the air as long they can. Players must kick the footbag once, passing it to their partner; then twice each; then three times; working up to five kicks. After five kicks they must work back down—four, three, two, one—then back up again, and so on in the same pattern. A point is awarded for each kick of the footbag and an additional point is awarded for each completed round (1, 2, 3, 4, 5, 4, 3, 2, 1). The rally is over when the footbag touches the ground or a foul occurs, or when the One-Up Five-Down pattern is broken.

Team

Three or more players try to keep the footbag in the air as long they can. Each player is allowed up to 5 consecutive kicks before passing the footbag. A point is awarded for each kick of the footbag. The rally is over when the footbag touches the ground or a foul occurs, or when one of the players makes more than 5 consecutive strikes of the footbag.

Other Footbag Games

Hackball

Modeled after 4-square, the only real difference is that you use a footbag for the ball and bouncing is not allowed. The footbag stays in the air as it is passed from square to square. Any part of the body may be used to strike the footbag. Each square should be about 3 feet x 3 feet (1 m x 1 m).

If a player fails to strike the footbag, and it lands in his square or goes out of bounds after he has touched it, he is out. The footbag must always be volleyed upward, if a player hits the footbag down at an opponent, he is out. A visibly upward motion must be imparted or the player who struck the footbag is out.

To make the game harder you can agree to use only the feet and legs for striking the footbag. In that case, larger squares would be recommended to maintain a safe distance between the players. If you wish, additional squares can be added to accommodate more players.

Copycat

Players arrange themselves in a circle. The first player makes a kick and then passes the footbag to the next player in the circle. That player must execute the same kick as the first player, then adds his own kick and passes the footbag on. Each successive player must copy the kicks that have gone before, in the sequence in which they were executed, and then adds his own and passes. The last player to execute the full sequence without an error wins the round and begins the next one. One point is awarded for each kick in the last successful sequence.

Round Robin

Players arrange themselves in a circle. The first player kicks the footbag once, the second one twice, the third three times, and so on. The player who completes the most consecutive kicks without a drop or a foul wins the round and is awarded one point for each successful kick.

Elimination

Players arrange themselves in a circle. The first player kicks the footbag as many times as he can. When he misses the footbag is passed to the next player who must make at least as many consecutive kicks as the first player to avoid elimination. He then adds as many kicks to that total as he can and gives the footbag to the next player. Each successive player must make as many or more kicks than his predecessor in order to avoid elimination. As each player is eliminated a new round begins with the next player in the circle. Play continues until there is only one player left.

Marbles

Although rooted in games that have been played for thousands of years, Marbles as we know it today came into being in the 1800s. The name is derived from the stone from which they were made, with the finest marbles fashioned from polished white alabaster. Less expensive marbles were made from clay, but were too easily chipped or broken. Experimentation led to the development of hand-made glass marbles, from which evolved their machine-made counterparts of today.

Lagging

The most common technique for determining the order of play is called lagging. Draw a shooting line and a lag line on the ground several feet apart, about 10 feet (3 m) is good if you have the room. Each player shoots one marble from behind the shooting line and tries to get it to stop as close as possible to the lag line. The closest shooter goes first in the game, next closest goes second, and so on.

Shooters and Mibs

The term *Shooter* is commonly used to refer to the marble that a player flicks with her thumb to try and hit other target marbles in the game, which are known as *Mibs*.

Funsies and Keepsies

Marbles games may be played *Keepsies*, with the winner actually getting to keep all of the marbles that were won during the game; or they may be played *Funsies* (also called *Friendlies*), where each player's original marbles are returned to her at the end of the game.

Ringer

1. Draw a circle on the ground 10 feet (3 m) across.

2. Put 13 mibs in the center of the circle arranged in a cross pattern and spaced three inches (8 cm) apart as shown in the diagram.

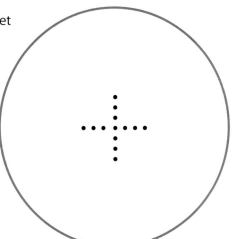

3. Each player shoots in turn from anywhere outside the large circle and tries to knock one or more mibs out of the circle.

4. If no mibs are knocked out of the circle the player's turn is over and the next player shoots.

5. If one or more mibs are knocked out of the circle but the player's shooter stops outside of the circle, the turn is over and the player keeps any mibs that were knocked out.

6. Players who knock out one or more mibs with the shooter staying in the ring get to shoot again from wherever the shooter stopped. They may continue shooting as long as on each shot one or more mibs is knocked out of the ring and the shooter stays in. When their shot fails to knock a mib out of the ring or their shooter ends up outside of the ring the turn is over. The player gets to keep all of the mibs knocked out during the turn.

7. Play continues with each player shooting in turn until all of the mibs are knocked out of the ring.

8. The player with the most mibs at the end of the game is the winner.

Ring Taw

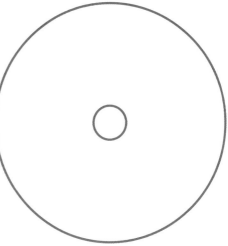

① Draw a circle on the ground about seven feet (2.1 m) across and draw a one foot (30 cm) circle in the middle of it.

② Each player puts the same number of mibs in the center circle (five is usually a good number).

③ In the first round each player shoots in turn from anywhere outside the large circle.

④ In subsequent rounds each player must shoot from wherever his shooter stopped.

⑤ If a player knocks a mib out of the inner circle he gets to keep that mib and continues to shoot. If no mibs are knocked out of the inner circle his turn is over.

⑥ If a player's shooter strikes another player's shooter during his shot that player must give him one of his marbles and the shooter gets to go again. He may not strike the same player's shooter twice in the same turn.

⑦ Play ends when there are no mibs left in the center circle.

⑧ The player with the most mibs is the winner.

Boss Out

❶ Draw a shooting line on the ground. The first player places a target marble, the boss, about 10 feet (3 m) from the shooting line.

❸ In turn, the players shoot at the boss from behind the line.

❹ If a player hits the boss he gets to keep it and all of the players who have shot pick up their shooters. The next player places a new boss and play begins again.

❺ If all players have shot once with no one hitting the boss, and no player's shooter has stopped within one giant step of the boss, all of the players pick up their shooters. The boss remains the same and play begins again with the first shooter.

❻ If there are one or more shooters within one giant step of the boss, all of those players can take a second shot at the boss by shooting bombsies (dropping the shooter on the boss from above waist level).

❼ All of the players who are more than one giant step from the boss pick up their marbles. Then the first bombsies shot is taken by the player who's shooter is closest to the boss.

❽ If a player hits the boss shooting bombsies he collects the boss and all the other marbles still on the ground. The next player places a new boss and play begins again.

❾ If no shooter hits the boss shooting bombsies all of the players pick up their shooters. The boss remains the same and play begins again with the first shooter.

❿ The game ends when a boss from each player has been played.

⓫ The player who has collected the most marbles wins.

Dropsies

1. Draw a square on the ground, about three feet (1 m) on each side.

2. Each player puts the same number of mibs in the square (five is usually a good number).

3. In turn, each player shoots bombsies from outside of the square and tries to knock one or more mibs out of the box.

4. Players may lean over the square while shooting it but cannot straddle its corners or any part of the box.

5. If no mibs are knocked out of the square the player's turn is over and the next player shoots.

6. If one or more mibs are knocked out of the square but the player's shooter rolls outside of the square, the turn is over and the player keeps any mibs that were knocked out.

7. Players who knock out one or more mibs with the shooter staying in the square get to shoot again. They may continue shooting as long as one or more mibs is knocked out of the square on each shot and the shooter stays in. When their shot fails to knock a mib out of the square or their shooter ends up outside of the square the turn is over. The player gets to keep all of the mibs knocked out during the turn.

8. Play ends when there are no mibs left in the square.

9. The player with the most mibs is the winner.

Potsies

1. Draw a circle on the ground 10 feet (3 m) across.

2. Each player puts the same number of mibs in the circle (five is usually a good number).

3. Arrange the mibs in a cross with the marbles spaced about three inches (8 cm) apart.

4. Each player shoots in turn from anywhere outside the circle and tries to knock one or more mibs out of the circle.

5. If no mibs are knocked out of the circle the player's turn is over and the next player shoots.

6. If one or more mibs are knocked out of the circle but the player's shooter stops outside of the circle, the turn is over and the player replaces any mibs that were knocked out, putting them as close as possible to the spot where they lay before they were struck.

7. Players who knock out one or more mibs with the shooter staying in the ring get to shoot again from wherever the shooter stopped. They may continue shooting as long as one or more mibs is knocked out of the ring on each shot and the shooter stays in. When their shot fails to knock a mib out of the ring or their shooter ends up outside of the ring the turn is over. The player gets to keep all of the mibs knocked out during the turn.

8. Play continues with each player shooting in turn until one of the players wins the number of mibs that they contributed.

9. That player is the winner and collects the entire pot.

Tic-Tac-Toe

❶ Draw a tic-tac-toe grid on the ground, making each square in the grid about two feet (61 cm) on a side.

❷ Draw a shooting line about five feet (1½ m) away from the grid.

❸ Each player gets one shot per turn from behind the shooting line and tries to get the marble to stop in one of the squares.

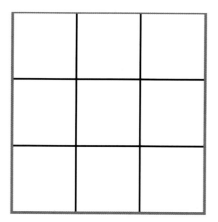

SHOOTING LINE

❹ The first marble in a square "owns" the square, and the only way for another player to take the square away is to knock that marble out.

❺ Any marble that stops in a square that is already occupied by another marble is picked up.

❻ The game ends when one of the players owns three squares in a row, down, across, or diagonally.

❼ There are no tie games. If all the opportunities to make three in a row are blocked, keep shooting until a marble is knocked out, freeing a square.

Jacks

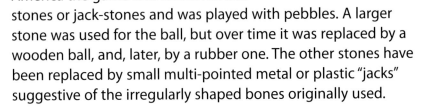

Various forms of the game of Jacks have been around for over 2000 years. Originally it was played with small stones or animal bones. In ancient Egypt it was played with sheep knuckle bones and in colonial America the game was known as five-stones or jack-stones and was played with pebbles. A larger stone was used for the ball, but over time it was replaced by a wooden ball, and, later, by a rubber one. The other stones have been replaced by small multi-pointed metal or plastic "jacks" suggestive of the irregularly shaped bones originally used.

Flipping

Flipping is the common way to determine who goes first in jacks games. Cup all of the jacks in two hands held together. Toss the jacks upward, and quickly turn your palms downward trying to catch as many of the jacks as you can on the backs of your hands. Now flip the jacks upward again while quickly turning your palms up and again catch as many of the jacks as you can in the palms of you hands. The player who drops the fewest jacks goes first, the one with the second fewest drops goes second, and so on. Ties are resolved by flipping again. If the players are so good at flipping that no one drops any jacks, you may increase the difficulty by trying the process one-handed.

Basic Jacks: Plainsies—Onesies, Twosies, etc.

❶ To start, throw the jacks on the floor.

❷ Throw the ball in the air, pick up the number of jacks required by the round, let the ball bounce once, and catch it before it bounces again. In the onesies round you pick the jacks up one at a time and repeat ten times. In the twosies round you pick up two at a time and repeat five times, and so on for threesies, foursies, etc., up to tensies, if you can. In any round where there are odd jacks leftover, like the single jack that's left in threesies, you pick up the leftover(s) on one final toss of the ball.

❸ You must use only one hand for throwing the ball, picking up the jacks, and catching the ball.

❹ You may not let the ball bounce twice.

❺ You may not drop the ball or any of the jacks that you have picked up.

❻ You may not move any of the other jacks on the ground except for the ones that you are picking up on that particular bounce. A little incidental contact is usually allowed, but if you are playing strictly by the rules—"strictsies"—you can't even touch them.

❼ Repeat until you have picked up all ten jacks.

❽ If you miss your turn is over. On your next turn you have to start over at the beginning of the turn in which you made your error.

Options to Make the Game Easier

You may allow any of the options below to make the basic game easier.

Cart

If you choose to pick up the leftovers before the final toss you are getting the "horse before the cart" and must call "cart" as you pick up the leftover jack(s).

Kissies or Haystacks

If two or more jacks are touching after your toss you may call "kissies" and pick up the jacks and throw them again. Likewise, if two or more jacks are entwined or atop one another, you may call "haystacks" and pick those jacks up and rethrow.

Overs

If you don't like the way the jacks land when you throw them you can call "overs" and pick them up and throw them again.

Split Jack

If the ball lands on a jack and takes a bad bounce, you can call "split jack" and pick up the ball and toss it again.

Fancies

Fancies are specialty variations on the basic jacks game.

Eggs in the Basket

1. Toss the ten jacks on the ground.

2. Bounce the ball, pick up one jack with the right hand and put it in the left hand—the basket. Count out loud "one" as you do so, and catch the ball before it bounces again.

3. Continue bouncing the ball, picking up jacks, transferring them to the basket, and catching while you count off each jack that is picked up.

4. If you pick up all of the jacks without a mistake, toss them out again and continue with eleven, and so on until a mistake is made.

5. The highest count reached is your score.

Pigs in the Pen

1. Form the "pig pen" by cupping your left hand on the ground with one side open to receive the jacks.

2. With your right hand, toss ten jacks on the ground.

3. Toss the ball in the air, sweep one of the jacks into the pig pen, and catch the ball before it bounces.

4. Repeat this until all of the jacks are swept into the pig pen.

5. Just as in Plainsies, you can work through onesies, sweeping one jack at a time into the pen; and then continue with twosies, sweeping two at a time; and on to threesies; and so on.

Scrubs

❶ Quickly slide the jacks back and forth on the ground with your right hand (scrubbing), and release the jacks to scatter them.

❷ Toss the ball, pick up one jack and scrub it back and forth, then catch the ball before it bounces.

❸ After the ball is caught the picked up jack can be transferred to the other hand.

❹ Then continue, tossing, picking up, scrubbing, and catching, until all of the jacks are picked up.

❺ Again, Scrubs can be played as onesies, twosies, threesies, and so on.

Sheep over the Fence

❶ Form the "fence" by putting your left hand and arm on the ground.

❷ With your right hand, toss ten jacks on one side of the fence.

❸ Toss the ball in the air, pick up one jack, place it on the other side of the fence, and catch the ball before it bounces. Don't throw the jacks, place them.

❹ Repeat this until all of the jacks are on the other side of the fence.

❺ Again, Sheep over the Fence can be played as onesies, twosies, threesies, and so on.

Goats on the Mountain

❶ Make the "mountain" by forming a fist with your hand on the ground.

❷ With your right hand, toss ten jacks on the ground.

❸ Toss the ball in the air and let it bounce. While the ball is in the air pick up one jack, place it on top of the mountain, and catch the ball before it bounces a second time.

❹ The first jack is pretty easy, but the mountain starts getting crowded pretty quickly. This becomes quite a delicate balancing act, but don't let the jacks fall of of the mountain.

❺ Repeat this until all of the jacks are balanced on top of your fist.

❻ If you'd like, you can reverse the game at this point, removing one goat from the mountain on each bounce of the ball.

❼ Again, Goats on the Mountain can be played as onesies, twosies, threesies, and so on.

Speed Jacks

❶ Toss ten jacks on the ground.

❷ Toss the ball, pick up one jack with the right hand and catch the ball.

❸ Toss the ball again, this time letting it bounce. Transfer the jack to the other hand, pick up another jack, and catch the ball before it bounces again.

❹ Continue the process—toss, transfer, pickup, and catch—until all of the jacks are in your left hand.

❺ Scatter them again and continue the game with twosies, threesies, and so on.

Marble Jacks

Play any of these games with the same rules as described here, but substitute marbles for the jacks. They are round and slippery and can make for a very difficult game.

Chinese Jump Rope

Chinese jump rope originated in 7th century China and remains popular today. A Chinese jump rope is a continuous loop of elastic cord. To play any Chinese jump rope game you will need at least three players. Two are the "enders" and one is the jumper. The jump rope is stretched around the enders. In the first round of a game it is stretched around one or both ankles of the enders. If the jumper completes the first round successfully it is moved up to the calves for the second round. In the third round it moves up to the knees. And finally, in the fourth round it moves up to the hips. You can try moving it higher if you'd like, but the games get more difficult as the rope moves up. Should the jumper miss at any point during the game she takes over for one of the enders who now has the opportunity to jump. A few of the common Chinese jump rope games follow, but once you get the hang of it, you should feel free to make up your own variations.

Americans

❶ Stretch the jump rope around both ankles of the enders. Stand next to the stretched rope.

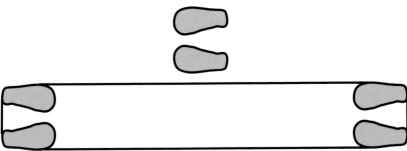

❷ Jump sideways so that you are straddling one side of the loop with your left foot in and your right foot out.

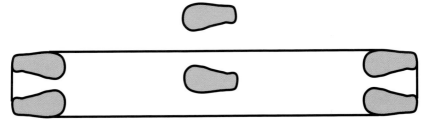

❸ Jump further sideways so that you are straddling the other side of the loop with your right foot in and your left foot out.

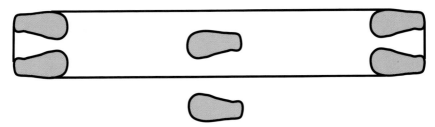

4 Jump back to straddle the right side of the loop…

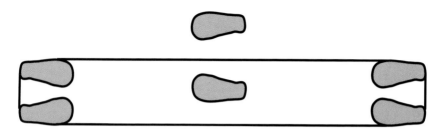

5 …and back again to straddle the left side.

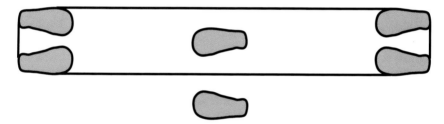

6 Jump inside the the ropes with your feet together.

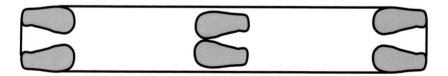

❼ Jump and spread your feet, stretching the ropes apart.

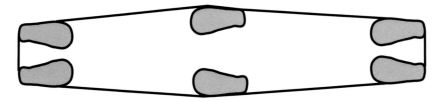

❽ Jump and bring your feet back together.

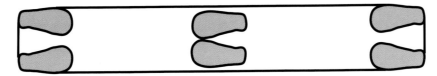

❾ Jump up and land with one foot on top of each rope.

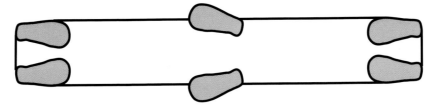

If you can complete these jumps without an error, move the rope up to calves and try again, then higher and higher after each successful round until you make a mistake.

Skinny Americans

❶ Stretch the jump rope around one ankle of each of the enders. Stand next to the stretched rope.

❷ Step in with your left foot, placing it between the closely spaced ropes.

❸ Sweep your foot out stretching the left rope away from you.

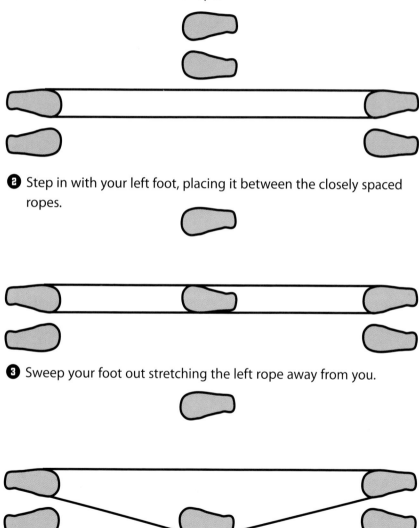

❹ Step in with your right foot . . .

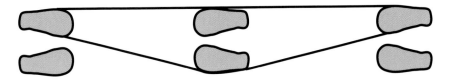

❺ . . . and out with your left.

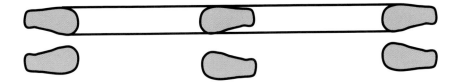

❻ Sweep out with your right foot stretching the right rope away.

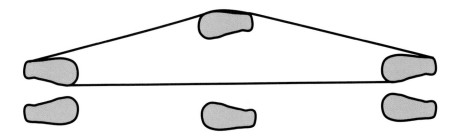

7 Step in with your left foot . . .

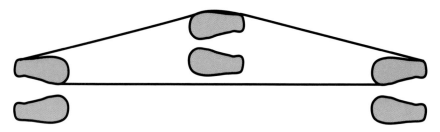

8 . . . and out with your right.

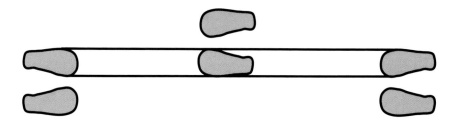

9 Repeat steps 3 through 5.

10 This time, when you step back in with your left foot keep you right foot in.

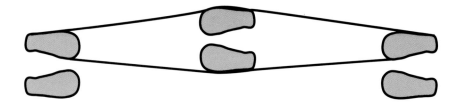

⓫ Jump and spread your feet, stretching the ropes apart.

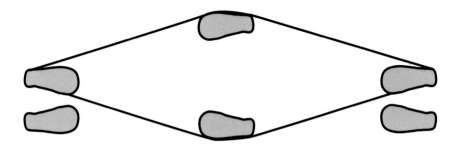

⓬ Jump and bring your feet back together.

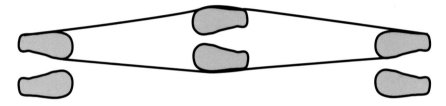

⓭ Jump up, turn, and land with both feet on top of both ropes.

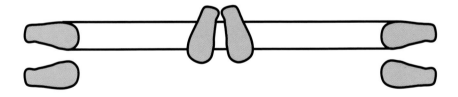

If you can complete these jumps without an error, move the rope up to calves and try again, then higher and higher after each successful round until you make a mistake.

Diamonds

❶ Stretch the jump rope around one ankle of each of the enders. Stand next to the stretched rope.

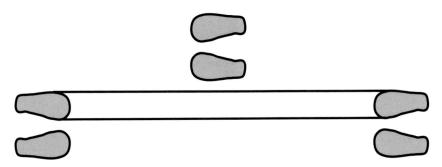

❷ With your left foot lift the closest rope over the farthest rope and put your foot down forming a diamond around it with the ropes.

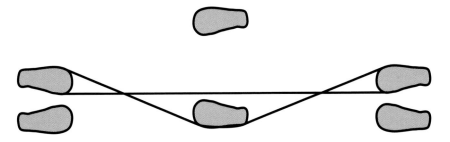

❸ Bring your other foot into the diamond and spread your feet apart.

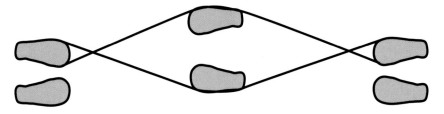

❹ Jump and spin so you are facing the opposite end. As you jump say "D," the first letter in diamond.

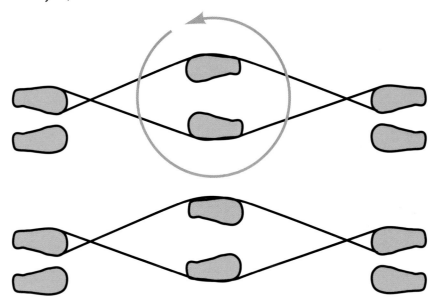

❺ Continue jumping and spinning spelling out an additional letter of the word D-I-A-M-O-N-D with each jump.

❻ Once you have spelled the word, jump up and bring your feet together.

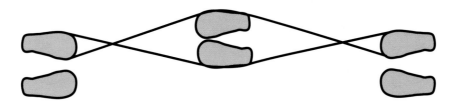

❼ Jump and spread your feet, stretching the ropes apart.

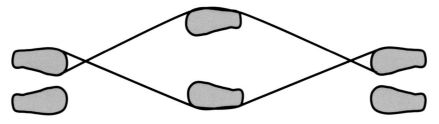

❽ Jump and bring your feet back together.

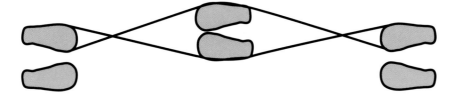

❾ Jump up, turn, and land with both feet on top of both ropes.

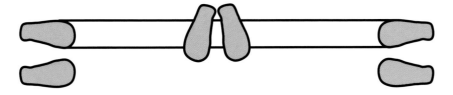

If you can complete these jumps without an error, move the rope up to calves and try again, then higher and higher after each successful round until you make a mistake.

Sailboats

❶ Stretch the jump rope around one ankle of each of the enders. Stand facing the stretched rope.

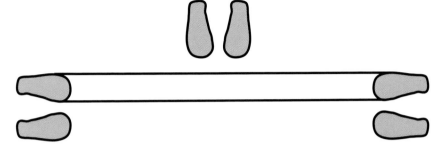

❷ With your right foot lift the closest rope over the farthest rope and put your foot down forming a diamond around it with the ropes.

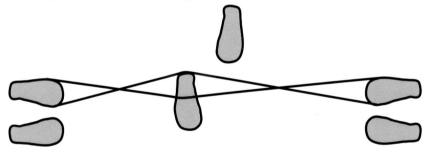

❸ With your left foot step in between the ropes to the left of the diamond.

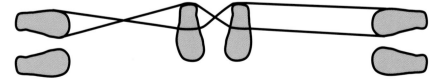

4 Jump and bring your left foot forward while bringing your right foot backward at the same time.

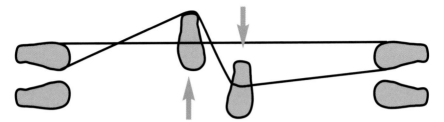

5 Jump and bring your right foot forward while bringing your left foot backward at the same time.

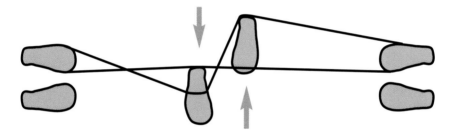

6 Jump and bring your left foot forward while bringing your right foot backward at the same time.

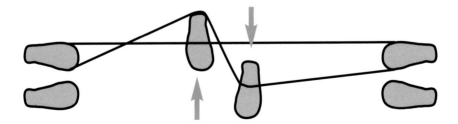

❼ Jump and bring your right foot forward while bringing your left foot backward at the same time.

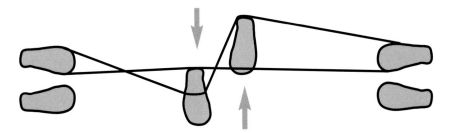

❽ Jump and land with your feet together.

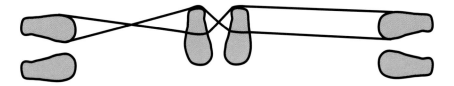

❾ Jump and spread your feet apart.

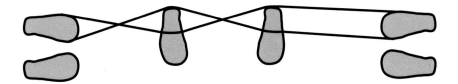

❿ Jump and bring your feet back together.

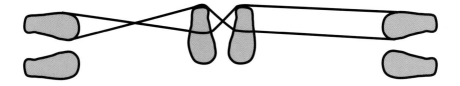

⓫ Jump up, and land with both feet on top of both ropes.

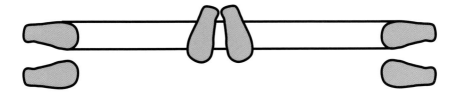

If you can complete these jumps without an error, move the rope up to calves and try again, then higher and higher after each successful round until you make a mistake.

Chinese

❶ Stretch the jump rope around both ankles of the enders. Stand next to the stretched rope.

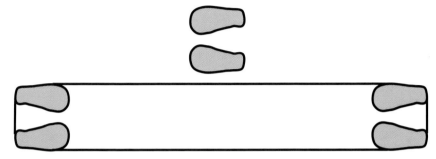

❷ Jump sideways so that you are straddling one side of the loop with your left foot in and your right foot out.

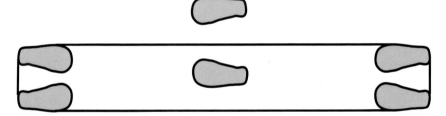

❸ Jump further sideways so that you are straddling the other side of the loop with your right foot in and your left foot out.

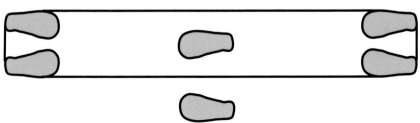

❹ Jump back to straddle the right side of the loop…

❺ …and back again to straddle the left side.

❻ Jump inside the the ropes with your feet together.

❼ Jump up and spread your feet, landing with both feet outside and straddling the ropes.

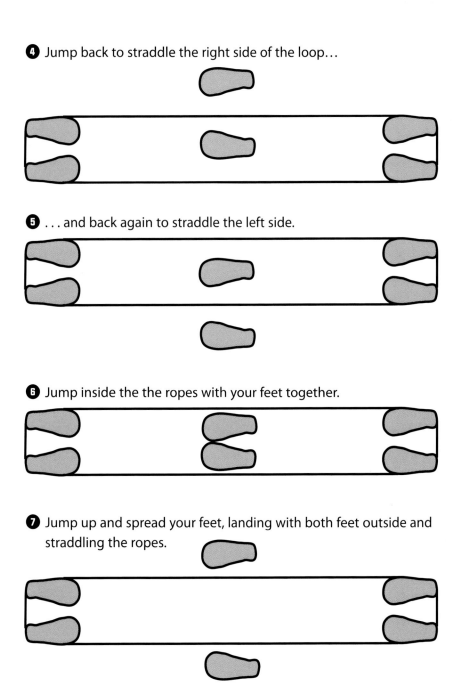

❽ Jump and bring your right foot in line in front of your left foot, crisscrossing the ropes.

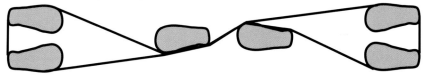

❾ Jump up and spread your feet, landing with both feet outside and straddling the ropes.

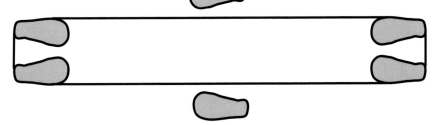

❿ Jump up and land with one foot on top of each rope.

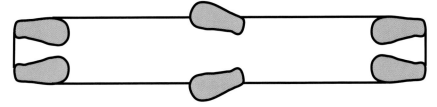

If you can complete these jumps without an error, move the rope up to calves and try again, then higher and higher after each successful round until you make a mistake.

Snap Back

❶ Stretch the jump rope around one ankle of each of the enders. Stand facing the stretched rope with your toes under the closest rope.

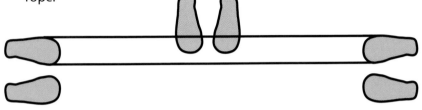

❷ Jump over the farthest rope lifting the closest rope with your toes so that you land inside a diamond formed by the ropes.

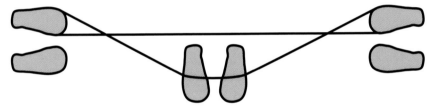

❸ Step back with your right foot stretching the rope behind you.

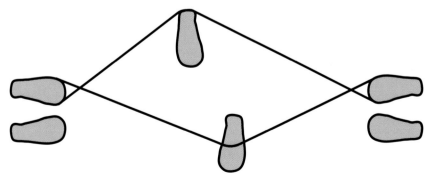

❹ Then step back with your left foot to bring it beside your right.

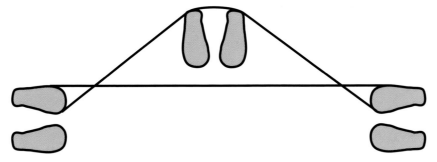

❺ Jump forward so that you land on both feet on the opposite side of the rope from where you started.

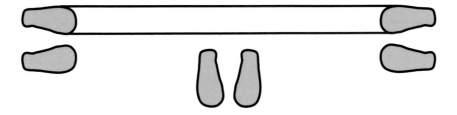

If you can complete these jumps without an error, move the rope up to calves and try again, then higher and higher after each successful round until you make a mistake. When you reach the knees you will have to begin by getting your knees under the rope before you first jump.

Tag & Other Fun Games

When we think of games today the mind turns usually to sporting goods stores full of equipment: balls, nets, bats, mallets, the list goes on and on. But many of the games that have amused children through the centuries require nothing more than a little ingenuity and imagination. If you listen for the sounds of children's laughter, you might find one of these games being played almost anywhere on the planet.

Picking Who Is "It"

Many games require a player to be declared "it" at the beginning of the game. Often rhymes are used to select who would be "it". The players form a circle facing each other and hold out a hand made into a fist. One player recites the rhyme, and with each word taps the fists around the circle in sequence. The last player tapped at the end of the rhyme is "it".

Some familiar rhymes are:

> Eeney, meeney, myney, moe / Catch a tiger by the toe
> If he hollers / let him go
> Eeney, meeney, myney, moe
> My mother told me to choose the very best one, and you are IT.

> Engine, engine, number nine / going down Chicago line
> If the train falls off the track, / do you want your money back?
> *(The player tapped picks yes or no and the word is then spelled out.)*
> N-O spells no / you don't get your money back.
> OR—Y-E-S spells yes / and you shall have you money back.

> Inka bink a bottle of ink, / the cork fell off and you do stink,
> Not because you're dirty, / not because you're clean,
> Just because you kissed a (boy or girl)
> Behind a magazine and you are IT.

The following rhyme selects "it" by eliminating players from the circle. As the rhyme goes around, each player who is tapped on the word "more" removes his fist, and the rhyme continues with the remaining players until only one fist is left.

> One potato, two potato, three potato, four.
> Five potato, six potato, seven potato, *more*.

Tag

1. Boundaries are declared for the area of play, so that players cannot run very far away to avoid being tagged.

2. One of the players is initially chosen to be "it."

3. The other players scatter throughout the playing area.

4. "It" chases after any or all of the other players in an attempt to tag one of them.

5. Upon being tagged that player will become the new "it," and the previous "it" joins the other players trying to avoid being tagged.

6. Play may continue indefinitely—there is no "winner" in basic tag. Players are considered to be better at tag if they can avoid being tagged, spending the least time being "it."

7. Often, one or more home bases will be declared to allow safe-haven where players may rest. Usually home is a tree, a pole, a bench, or some other object within the field of play. While touching home base a player cannot be tagged. Players may generally only spend an limited amount of time at the base to rest. It is not meant to be a place to linger just to avoid being tagged.

8. Sometimes players are considered to be safe if they are touching a player who is touching the base, a condition referred to as "electricity."

9. Usually the player being tagged must allow the person tagging them an opportunity to get away from them before attempting to tag them back. Sometimes the tagger must declare "no tag backs," in order to be granted temporary immunity from being tagged.

Grab Tag

1. Boundaries are declared for the area of play, so that players cannot run very far away to avoid being tagged.

2. One of the players is initially chosen to be "it."

3. The other players scatter throughout the playing area.

4. "It" chases after any or all of the other players in an attempt to tag one of them.

5. In this variation on tag it is best for "it" to try tag one of the other players on a difficult to reach spot because . . .

6. . . . the tagged player becomes the new "it" AND must grab the spot where he was tagged and keep his hand on that spot while chasing after and trying to tag another player. If the player has been tagged in an awkward place the chase can be quite comical.

7. Play may continue indefinitely. Players are considered to be better at tag if they can avoid being tagged, spending the least time being "it."

Freeze Tag

1. Boundaries are declared for the area of play, so that players cannot run very far away to avoid being tagged.

2. One of the players is initially chosen to be "it."

3. The other players scatter throughout the playing area.

4. "It" chases after any or all of the other players in an attempt to tag one of them.

5. Upon being tagged a player must freeze in the position in which they were tagged until they are tagged again and "unfrozen" by one of the other players who is not "it".

6. The goal is for "it" to freeze all of the players. This can be very difficult, since she must not only chase and freeze every player but must also keep them from unfreezing each other in the process.

7. If she can manage to freeze all of the players, the round is over and she gets to select the next "it".

Pie Tag

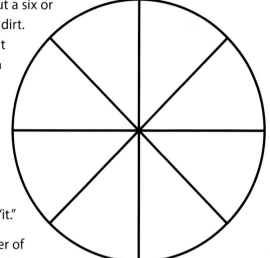

❶ The players scratch out a six or eight piece pie in the dirt. If played on pavement the pie may be drawn with chalk. The pie should be quite large—15 or 20 feet (4½–6 m) across would be good.

❷ One of the players is initially chosen to be "it."

❸ "It" stands at the center of the pie and the other players spread out around the edge.

❹ "It" shouts out "GO" and chases after a player trying to tag him.

❺ "It" and all of the players may only run along the lines that make up the pie shape.

❻ If a player leaves the lines they are immediately declared the new "it".

❼ If a player is tagged they become the new "it".

❽ Play may continue indefinitely. Players are considered to be better at tag if they can avoid being tagged, spending the least time being "it."

❾ For interesting variations you can try playing on shapes other than the pie. Be creative and make up your own playing board.

Rabbit

❶ Players select an area for the "rabbit hutch"—this will be a safe home base during the game.

❷ One of the players is initially chosen to be the "hunter"—this game's version of "it".

❸ All of the other players are the "rabbits" and the gather in the hutch where they are safe from the hunter.

❹ The hunter stands 20 feet (6 m) away from the hutch and selects one rabbit to come out and stand at least 10 feet (3 m) away from the hutch. During the game one of the rabbits must be out of the hutch at all times.

❺ The game starts with a count: "One-Two-Three-GO."

❻ On "GO", the hunter chases after and tries to tag the rabbit that is outside the hutch.

❼ That rabbit may run into the hutch for safety, but when she enters the hutch she must touch one of the other rabbits who must then leave the hutch and try to avoid being tagged.

❽ If the hunter tags a rabbit, that rabbit becomes the new hunter, the old hunter enters the hutch becoming one of the rabbits and selects another rabbit to leave the hutch and be hunted.

Octopus

1. Boundaries are declared for the area of play—the "ocean". There should be two clearly defined "shores" of the ocean, opposite each other.

2. One of the players is initially chosen to be the "octopus"—this game's version of "it".

3. The octopus stands in the middle of the ocean.

4. The other players are the "fish" and line up on one shore of the ocean.

5. When the octopus shouts "swim" the fish must try to cross the ocean to the opposite side while the octopus tries to tag them.

6. Any fish that the octopus tags join hands with him and become tentacles of the octopus. They then try to tag other fish and join them to the octopus.

7. In each round there will be fewer fish and a larger and larger octopus until only one fish is left.

8. That player is the winner and chooses the octopus for the next game.

Hide and Seek

1. Boundaries are declared for the area of play, so that players cannot go very far away to hide and avoid being found.

2. One of the players is initially chosen to be "it."

3. "It" stands in the middle of the playing area with his eyes closed and counts aloud to one hundred.

4. The other players scatter to find hiding spots throughout the playing area.

5. When "it" finishes counting, he searches the playing area trying to find any of the hidden players.

6. When one of the hiding players is found they become the new "it" for the next round. "It" shouts out "Allie, Allie, Oxen free" and all the other players come out of their hiding places.

7. As a variation, "it" may continue to search until all of the players are found before the next round is started.

8. Then the last player to be found is the winner and gets to select the new "it".

Arm Wrestling

❶ Two players sit facing each other at a table

❷ They place their elbows on the table and clasp their right hands palm to palm as shown here.

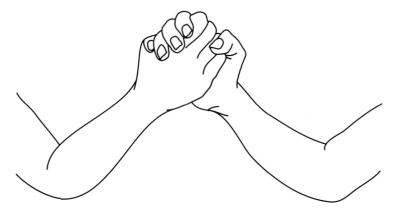

❸ The match starts with a count: "One-Two-Three-GO."

❹ On "GO," each player tries to push the other's hand down so that the back of the hand touches the table.

❺ The player who forces the other's hand back until it is all the way down is the winner.

❻ This game should only be played by two players of relatively equal strength.

Hand Wrestling

❶ Two players stand facing each other and place their right feet together on the ground side-by-side and touching heel to toe.

❷ They grasp each other's right hand and set themselves to be balanced and ready to begin.

❸ The match starts with a count: "One-Two-Three-GO."

❹ On "GO," each player tries to push or pull on the others hand to make his opponent lose his balance.

❺ The object is to make your opponent move one of his feet, stumbling or stepping out of his starting position.

❻ Pushing your opponents body to force him off balance is not allowed.

❼ The player who can make his opponent lose his balance while maintaining his own is the winner.

Marco Polo

1. The area of play for this game is a swimming pool.
2. One of the players is initially chosen to be "it."
3. The other players position themselves throughout the pool.
4. "It" is *blind* for this game (for safety a blindfold is not recommended in a pool, so generally "it" simply keeps her eyes closed).
5. In this variation on tag "it" must locate the other players by sound.
6. Whenever "it" calls out "Marco," all of the other players must respond "Polo".
7. "It" follows the sound of the responding players to locate and tag one.
8. When a player is tagged they become "it" for the next round.
9. Play may continue indefinitely. Players are considered to be better at tag if they can avoid being tagged, spending the least time being "it."

Duck Duck Goose

❶ Players form a circle with all sitting down and facing each other.

❷ One of the players is initially chosen to be "it."

❸ The "it" player walks around the circle tapping the seated players' heads and declaring each to be a "duck" or a "goose" as they go.

❹ When he declares someone to be the "goose", that player gets up and chases the "it" player around the circle.

❺ "It" tries to get all of the way around and take the goose's spot in the circle before the goose can tag him.

❻ If the goose can't catch him, he takes the goose's place in the circle, the goose becomes "it", and the next round begins.

❼ If the goose does catch up and tags him before he can get there, he must sit in the middle of the circle, the goose becomes "it", and the next round begins.

❽ A player who goes to the middle of the circle must stay there until another player is tagged and takes his place.

Mother May I

❶ Players form a line facing in the same direction.

❷ One player takes the position of the "mother," standing at a distance from the line of players and facing away from them.

❸ The mother randomly calls a player from the line, and gives her an instruction.

❹ The form of the instruction is:

"(player's name), you may take (some number) giant/regular/baby steps forward/backward."

For example: "Betsy, you may take three giant steps forward."

❺ She would then reply with the question, "Mother, may I?"

❻ The mother would then respond with "yes" or "no."

❼ The player follows the instruction if the answer is yes, or remains in place if the answer is no.

❽ If the player forgets to ask "Mother, may I?" she must go back to her starting position.

❾ The first player to reach the mother takes her place and the next round begins.

The following variation allows the game to be played with a group of children who are not familiar with each other's names.

❶ The players take turns asking, "Mother may I take . . . steps?"

❷ The mother replies yes or no.

❸ The player takes the step(s) if the answer is yes, or remains in place if the answer is no.

Red Light — Green Light

❶ Players form a line facing in the same direction.

❷ One of the players is initially chosen to be "it."

❸ "It" stands at a distance of thirty to fifty feet from the line of players and faces away from them.

❹ "It" shouts out "green light" and *silently* counts to ten, he may count slowly or quickly.

❺ While "it" is counting the other players may move toward him.

❻ When "it" reaches ten, he shouts out "red light" and spins around quickly to look at the players.

❼ The players must all freeze in position when they hear "red light"—if "it" sees any of them still moving when he turns around he sends them back to the start line.

❽ Then "it" shouts "green light" and turns away to count again.

❾ The first player to reach "it" is the winner of that round and becomes the new "it" for the next round.

Blind Man's Bluff

1. Boundaries are declared for the area of play so that players cannot go very far away to avoid being found. It is best to use an enclosed area like a large room or a fenced yard. The area should be free of hazardous obstructions that someone could trip over or bump into and be hurt.

2. One of the players is initially chosen to be "it."

3. The other players position themselves throughout the playing area. They are free to move about during the game.

4. "It" is *blind* for this game, a blindfold may be used, or "it" may simply keep his eyes closed.

5. "It" gropes about trying to tag any of the other players. Players may attempt to distract and confuse it by making funny noises or calling out taunts.

6. If "it" tags one of them she must stand still while "it" feels her face and tries to identify her.

7. If "it" is successful in identifying her, she becomes the new "it" and the next round begins.

8. If not, the game continues until some player is found and identified.

9. In one variation on the game "it" does not need to identify the tagged player, simply tagging them makes them the new "it" and the next round begins.

10. Play may continue indefinitely. Players are considered to be better at Blind Man's Bluff if they can avoid being tagged, spending the least time being "it."

Red Rover

❶ Players form two teams.

❷ The teams line up facing each other 15 to 20 feet (4½–6 m) apart.

❸ Members on each team clasp hands to form a human chain.

❹ Team one calls out "Red Rover, Red Rover, will (name of a player from team two) come over."

❺ The player who's name is called runs across to the chain formed by team one team and tries to break through.

❻ If she succeeds, she may choose one of the players on team one to bring back to team two.

❻ If she does not succeed, she joins team one and the next round begins.

❼ Team two then calls out "Red Rover, Red Rover, will (name of a player from team one) come over," and that player must try to break through the chain formed by team two.

❽ Play continues, alternating between teams, until all of the players have been absorbed into one long chain.

Note: Players should be cautioned against using excessive force during this game, as injuries could result. Some adult supervision is strongly recommended. Players should not be allowed to swing their hands or arms at the human chain in their attempt to break through. They should only run at the spaces between the opposing players—not directly at any one of them. Rough play must be discouraged.

Simon Says

❶ This is a game for three or more players: the more players, the better the game.

❷ One of the players is initially chosen to be "Simon"—this game's version of "it".

❸ All of the other players line up facing "Simon". If there are many players, they may line up several rows deep.

❹ Simon commands the players to perform certain tasks, and while giving the command "Simon" demonstrates it. For example:

"Simon says, touch your toes."—while Simon touches his toes
"Simon says, hop on one foot."—while hopping on one foot
Even, *"Simon says do this"*—while demonstrating "this"

❺ The players must follow Simon's command as long as Simon begins it with the words "Simon says . . ."

❻ If a player fails to promptly follow a command that begins with "Simon says. . . " Simon declares them to be out and they must leave the game.

❼ Simon may also give some commands that leave out the required "Simon says . . ."

❽ If a player follows a command that does NOT begin with "Simon says . . ." Simon declares them to be out and they leave the game.

❾ Play continues until there is only one player remaining. They are the winner and get to be "Simon" for the next round.

Rock – Paper – Scissors

❶ This is a game for two players only.

❷ The two players face each other, hands behind their backs.

❸ Together they count to three and, on three each present a hand in one of three shapes"

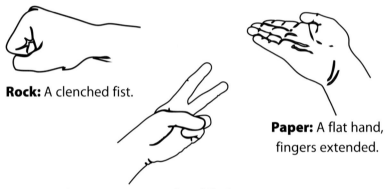

Rock: A clenched fist.

Paper: A flat hand, fingers extended.

Scissors: Pointer and middle finger extended in a "vee" shape.

❹ The combination determines who is the winner as follows:

If Rock and Scissors: Rock smashes Scissors, Rock wins.

If Scissors and Paper: Scissors cut Paper, Scissors wins.

If Paper and Rock: Paper wraps Rock, Paper wins.

❺ If both players choose the same shape, the round is declared a tie and they play again.

❻ Players may keep score and play until an agreed upon goal is reached to declare a winner.

❼ This game can also be used as a selection method in other games, similar to the way a coin toss is used, but requiring no equipment.